THE TURN AROUND
BETWEEN
RICKY AND JEANIE
"WHEN GOD'S LOVE CHANGED OUR LIVES"

Jeanie Breedwell

Author's Tranquility Press

MARIETTA, GEORGIA

Copyright © 2022 by Jeanie Breedwell.

All rights reserved. No part of this publication may be reproduced, distributed or transmitted in any form or by any means, including photocopying, recording, or other electronic or mechanical methods, without the prior written permission of the publisher, except in the case of brief quotations embodied in critical reviews and certain other noncommercial uses permitted by copyright law. For permission requests, write to the publisher, addressed "Attention: Permissions Coordinator" at the address below.

Jeanie Breedwell/Author's Tranquility Press
2706 Station Club Drive SW
Marietta, GA 30060
www.authorstranquilitypress.com

Ordering Information:
Quantity sales. Special discounts are available on quantity purchases by corporations, associations, and others. For details, contact the "Special Sales Departmen" at the address above.

The Turn Around Between Ricky and Jeanie/Jeanie Breedwell
Paperback: 978-1-958554-05-0
eBook: 978-1-958554-06-7

My story started in 2006 after I lost my husband and one month later lost my baby daughter from an overdose of pills.

My world was turned upside down, God was the one I leaned on and I was so glad to be part of my late husband's life to lead him to Jesus; he got saved on his deathbed. I will tell you I was sad, but I did not let it get me down. I went to church and keep my mind on the one who loved me & the one who died for me. I did not lose hope in my future; it just took me some time to move on with my life. I miss my family. I did cry lots of tears thinking about my daughter and my late husband. This went on for three years.

One day, some friends of mine were having lunch and I wanted to move on just so I could turn my life around, love someone else and have a future. That is when Ricky came into my life. At the time, I was so happy we went to the movies. I felt like we were the only ones on earth. He was so nice to me and when my phone rang, I knew it was my shining armor calling me. It was something about him that made me feel like a queen. I was so afraid to close my eyes that I might be dreaming. We had fun days together; l love to hear him laugh. The ones I was having lunch with arranging dinner for Ricky and me, I was nervous. He was the first one I had dated and for over three years, he did not talk too much, but he was nice to me.

I noticed he was drinking beer, and I thought maybe this is not what God wanted. After all, we dated a few times and it just so happens he got fired from his job, the place he lived was the one he worked for and he had to move out. Other things were against us and I told him to not worry. I had someone l wanted him to meet, friends of mine, Jerry and Sue Farmer and we were on our way to Wildwood.

The other part of my life, I have known them for a long time, my children and their daughter Cindy were close friends.

They liked Ricky, we began doing things together and we talked about God. Ricky knew that they were Christian people and I do not think he was around too many people outside of the ones that introduced us to each other.

I know what we did living together was wrong, but he made me feel like a different person the way he treated me while we were together. I told him I love the Lord, went to church; my mom brought me up that way. If he wanted me as his wife, then he would go with me to church. Sorry to say it, but the way he loved me took my eyes off the Lord when we were together. I felt so alive in his loving arms. Ricky could make you feel that way. I never met anyone that made me change my mind; it was different with him.

Back to the time with my friends Jerry and Sue called me and said that they had found us a house.

Ricky, I think said, "All right" sometimes that was his phrase when he was happy. He turned the van around and off to the new place we went. Jerry and Sue knew the owner and we looked at the house with our friends and checked every room. It had two bedrooms and as we walked into the kitchen, off to our right was another small room. I like the kitchen. It had lots of room for my dishes, pots, pans and can also store other things. Out in the backyard, we can place our washer and dryer when we get one.

We had set a date for our wedding plans, we paid down on the rent for the month and went back to the motel until we could move as I was staying with my daughter at the time, so we had to go there to get to my things.

I did not have too many things to move, so I made everything simple, just myself, the dog, and I brought someone with me to care of my dog.

Ricky had a small red truck so I put the things of mine in boxes so I could move them without having trouble when I got to our first home. I did have a few tables we had to bring into our new home. We had no beds so we made our way to Walmart to get some blow-up beds, which before morning we both found ourselves on the floor. We had to do that every time so we could go to bed until we could get us some new things for our new house. We did finally get the house in order, bought something we did not have in our kitchen and made plans for our wedding in May. We also went to church with our friends until that special day we were to get married. Ricky thinks we're still in the trailer where he lived when I met him. He was still drinking when we got together. I did not like it, but I went along with it. I prayed to God to take it away from him. He was working with one of his friends in Plymouth, so he would get up early to get to work because where he worked was about one hour away. As our wedding got closer, we began to get ready for it. I had Ricky to drive me to get me a wedding dress, he did not go in. I picked my wedding dress out; it was so pretty but it was so long when I tried it on.

The lady in the store helped me, she knew it was too long so I carried it to someone that knew what to do since there were some things that needed to be fixed before my wedding day. It cost so much and it was still down to my feet. I had other things to get like a shoe and a bra.

Anyway, we had help with our wedding. Ricky asked Jerry Farmer to be his best man and my girls were at the wedding as I needed them. I had a flower girl and someone to bring the ring.

Everything played out before the wedding. My niece did my hair and makeup and did a good job. I played our wedding song I wrote, and we had our family and friends there. It was one of the happy days of my life. We laughed and had so much fun! and we both got cake on us just as I had planned. Our pastor performed our wedding and we went to the motel for our honeymoon for a couple of days, then back to our little house as Mr. and Mrs. Ricky Dobbs.

He was working with a friend close by, so I had my weeks planned out. Getting up in the morning making his breakfast and lunch, then the day was mine to do what I needed to do. He missed me as I missed him because he would ring my number just to say I love you, to make my day. He worked for a while at that job, and moved on to another one. Rick was a hard worker that people liked him so much. He worked every day he could. We did have good times together after we got our computer and I thought about my daughter Alice, she had been on my mind for some time. I was crying every day, wanting to do something to help me to go on. Ricky was there for me, putting his arms around me to comfort me while I cried. He was so concerned about what I was going through, that he tried many things to settle my mind like putting things together and digging a hole buried it in our backyard.

It did not help, so we thought about calling our pastor, where we attend church to see if we could get the ones at our church to come to our house and we would have a funeral service for Alice and made it happen. We set the date, they came, friends and family came, it was heart breaking. Ricky stepped in and comforted me once again. We got a picture of Alice buried in the backyard. I said a poem that I had written for her. I could not hold the tears back. The pastor prayed for me as well like the ones attending the service.

Ricky likes going to church, we live over an hour away yet we still went there no matter what the weather was. One day, Ricky and I were talking about writing a book on Alice. He said I know what to name it, "Assassination by Doctor". Yes, I said that's a good name, so I got online to put my dream as a vocation to make Alice's life come alive again with what I remember as a baby that God had given me. I said she belonged in a doll house because she was so pretty. I talked to someone and they said the book sounded good, but the price was out of reach. We would have to pay an amount that was high but Ricky and I wanted Alice's story out there. He put a few words about why we were writing her book. Ricky was an amazing person, he had dedication that I did not have and he knew what to say, so he helped me write her book.

He never saw Alice, but the way he talked would make you wonder. He grabbed every word I said and he listened to what I feel.

God was with us will us getting married in May. Our friends Sue and Jerry Farmer, we invited to our first Christmas in our new home. Ricky and I got everything together. I cooked a big turkey and ham, the table was big, so we had plenty of room to place things. I had put a bowl of fruit on there, we had a tree decorated for Christmas, we were to enjoy Jerry and Sue were right on time. They stayed a bit with us after we prayed and ate, we insisted they carry some food home, and we all had a good Christmas present for everyone. It is good to have friends over to have Christmas dinner. The most important thing is because of what it is all about - Christ's birthday that year. The year was ending, we were ready for 2010, Ricky was still working at his new job, he was really small, so my work was ahead of me to cook good food. He did gain weight, then he backed off from eating so much, his pants were getting tight, but lol, he liked my cooking. We had stayed in our greenhouse for a while then one day, I was on my computer. I do not know how it came about, but I wanted to get in touch with my cousin. We all lived in Alabama as kids growing up, so I did not remember his name; we all call him Ray. So, I had to call my brother because he knew his name and

I googled it on my computer, and his name came up. To make the story short, I called his number, we made plans to go to Alabama to meet him in one of the motels in Scotts born. It took us forever to find our way, no signs to find our way but with the good Lord on our side, we made it to the motel where I was to meet my cousin after fifty years.

When we were little kids playing in my yard, we talked and followed him to his brother's house. At one time, my aunt lived with him, and he wanted us to move in with him.

It was not what Ricky and I wanted, so with the praying and the church backing us up, we did not want to leave.

While we made up our minds, we had our friends Sue and Jerry step in looking for a place for us. Here at the motel, Ricky and I started our little lives here, and we moved here in 2012, we have gone through so much that we picked up where we left off finding us a church.

Sue calls me one day telling me about the church we have been going to for 6 years. We like it like the people the pastor Gary Bunn, his sweet wife sister Beth Bunn, his father George Bunn, Terry Beth, and the Yvette Bunn. They all love the Lord and the pastor knows how to preach the word of God, we've only been there a few weeks when we joined the church and we liked it that much that Ricky started to change his things in life though it took him a while but he was faithful to go to church.

We left our place early and stay for a while before church began. I could tell Ricky like the people of the church he loved them to it was our home away from home. If they had something they wanted him to help with anything, he was there on time sometimes he joined them on Saturday morning for breakfast with the men.

George Bunn he was over that, Ricky liked that he would ask me if he could bring me something back sometimes, I said yes most of the time I just wanted him to be with the men to forget me while he enjoyed his time with his friends, maybe he liked that. He sure did like the pastor; they laughed about some things they did have things in common, December the 21st, they shared their birthdays. Ricky did the grocery shopping and if he was on his way home from work, he would call me to see if I needed anything. He was good about it that if it was bad weather, I would worry about him I would tell him just come on home. He was all right with that. I know he was tired so he would just stay on that same road to our place we did have our up and downs like all married couples do.

Sometimes I would bust the bubble, I would go to him tell him l was sorry. I was standing in front of a person when we first met. He was different, he would not give in, he was set in his ways. I was told we would not stay together not even a year, it all depends on how you treat a person.

No one likes to be told they cannot do anything.

I believe what was wrong with Ricky. I remember he told someone he had met, you have got to be good to people in order to want them to listen to you, tell them about Jesus. They had got to know who you let lead you before we got married. I told Ricky I was a born-again Christian and I did attend church and I wanted him to go with me. He said he would want that and that made me happy many times. He went and I stayed in the room, I could tell he was changing his life for the good I think Ricky did not understand the real Bible. He did not have a Bible when I met him. Never saw him read one. His life was in another direction but a little love you show him and it turns him the right way. He was looking for love in all the wrong places. I think he was starving for love that was what's wrong with him. He did have good parents and Grandma, I read cards and letters they all sent him at birthday and Christmas and sometimes just to say they love him they were heart breaking he had pictures of all through the years from the time he was born and of his family all pass away.

When Ricky was still young, I think it did a number on his life to lose his whole family. Ricky got another job in the village not too far from the motel where we lived at a golf course. He liked it so much never was late to sign in. The only one time I remember he did not go to work God was with him when it happened in 2013. When he had his appendix burst, he said he knew when it happened but it never hurt, so he was at home for a while, then he had to give in and go to the hospital. He was there for around two weeks I only got to call him, he said it was okay. I wanted to be with him but I could not we have gone. We have spent so much time together since we first we left the house, where we started our little nest of love for each other, I call it the green house. We were there for almost two years that is where we started Alice back in 2009, we did not want to go to Alabama but my special cousin wanted us to take care of his brother, and I did not want to let him down so we went leaving everything behind until we could move. When we found out where we would stay when we got there it was okay, but I felt like I had made a mistake. It did not feel right but my cousin paid the way for us.

Then I felt bad for Ricky, I knew he did not want to be there; he just wanted to please me. I think I remember one time my best friend Sue Farmer told me he would go anywhere with me. You know I think she was right back to our place of when we got together, Wildwood Florida. Ricky went back to work after the hospital. After some love and care from me, he was back to work. He would work his hours and go back at home. He was getting ready to face the old age coming his way after working so many years. Not saying he did not like the job he did and his co-workers, but l knew he was getting ready to retire. He was there for me one morning. I had my stomach hurt; this was in 2017. He went to the hospital and was right there with me; I was hurting so much for a few hours. He did not leave me until they gave me something to ease the pain. God healed me. Then when I saw a change in him, he took care of me after the hospital. I was in there for a long time before that I had my stomach to hurt, he would hear me crying, he would come to me to put his arms around me to make me feel better. God healed me in 2013 and after 7 years of hurting, we could be going somewhere and my stomach would start hurting he would find me a store where he would go in buy me a jar of pickle juice to help; he was the one told me to drink it.

Over the years, Ricky seemed to change his way of living, getting close to God, he was doing things I thought I had married a new person. God took over his life, he was a new man he loved the church and the people, but one day in 2018 was the sad time he started out with his leg hurting. He never complained much, we went to church and he would get groceries, I know he never felt like it but he did it for me. We did not know what it was. Finally, one day he went to the doctor. Here comes my world falling down. I could not believe it; he was hurting so much. I was devastated to hear him in so much pain. They treated him and to see the reaction, that made it worse if I knew what was going to do to my man, I would have put a stop to it and talked him out of it. Too much pain for one person to go through. While we had angels watching over us, they all chipped in and helped Rick and me get him to the doctor for his treatments just for a few names' sister Beth our pastor wife and a very sweet sister of the church her last name is Bunn, she is sent from heaven to help people. She was there for Rick and me she drove him to his treatment. I cannot say enough about her just a wonderful person. Now there are more that help us George Bunn and his three daughter Terry Bunn, she was there for us to bring Rick and me to church.

When he had to give up his driving because cancer got so bad, he was in so much pain, then there was Beth Bunn and Yevette Bunn, they all did what they could and the church was there for us Pastor Gary Bunn. He was the number one in Ricky's life. They were close friends and brothers in Christ.

We were all as a big family helping one another as we could. I watched my side husband for six months, hurting. It was so bad that he had to go places in a wheelchair. He could not walk in the last months of his life but believe it or not he made his way to church in pain. I would ask him to go home his reply was no, he wanted to be in church, I looked at people that won't go to church for little to nothing pain, but my husband wanted to go. He also did other things for the church. I remember Terry Bunn's statement about Rick coming to church; she said it touched her heart with the things Rick said and how he changed his life.

I want my readers to know that Ricky made his turn around before cancer. I give God the credit and the people at our church. Ricky did suffer so much but God was with him and we all need to take this at heart. Church is a place to be and Rick put that into action that you should always go to the church, we would be better. Turns outs if people saw how my husband wanted to know Jesus more, love him with all his heart and soul and body. My book has everything about what my husband wanted in his life; it was Jesus. I'm so happy to be part of the man who love God more than anything. He made my life better when he gave it all to the one who died for him. Instead of getting better, he got worse. They can't carry him to his treatment and he was having so much pain.

A week before he passed, they carried him to the hospital just down the road from us that was on Friday. One of the sisters brought me to see him. He told me they were getting him ready for a hip replacement down north somewhere. I thought things was working out for him. Before we got to the house, they came and got him pastor Gary Bunn and sister Beth Bunn came. We were on our way to the hospital took about two hours. We arrived there and spent some time with him. He was ready to go to his new home in heaven. He told me he was just hanging on. They told me I could stay as long as I wanted, they would wait but I knew they were tired, so they brought me home. Pastor went back to stay with him, good man of God. A few days later, the doctor call me and said, he was not any better. He wanted to tell me bye and he loves me. The doctor put the phone to his ear and told him what I said that was our last conversation to each other. He passed away on April 3rd, 2019. It has been a year ago, I miss him so much that it took a hold of me. The pastor helped me and all my family and friends. I love them all.

This is my story about a wonderful man that turned his life around for good. He saw sunshine instead of rain in his last days on earth. My husband Ricky Dobbs his story is in heaven with Jesus; I will see him one day.

End

Since Ricky has been gone, it has been rough on me. God has helped me through the bad times. He has had some of his angels carry me to get groceries and church when it happens. I was not ready to face the world. I cried all the time that after I was feeling better, my daughter, who had been fighting cancer for some time, lost her battle on October 12th, 2019. She went home to be with Jesus. Her children said she was smiling when she left this world. She had so much pain. Jesus once again was my comforter and was there for me to lean on. That was the only way I could make more tears to cry I did go stay with my daughter for a while. When this COVID-19 started, I was with her to help because they had closed some places and no money was coming in. I think it was a couple of months then back to where I have lived in for the last 8 years in a different room, I like it because it is roomier than the other. I live in I have a good friend that helps me, Becky, she brings me my mail and helps me in other ways.

God was my Leader from birth

MIRACLE OF GOD

Jeanie Breedwell

When I was a little girl in Alabama in the north of the state, my mother told my brother and me about Jesus. She told us many stories, and we were just sitting around the fireplace. That is what we do. Look at the fire burning in the old fireplace.

Mama told us about the one who died for us.

Mama was like an open book. She would open her mouth out and it would sometimes come that she would talk for a long time.

She had so much to feed usher kids with the word of God;

And since that was the only thing we knew, it was a tradition in our home. My Mama loves us, her kids.

She carried us to the old country Church. We had to walk to church with no car.

A friend of Mama told me she carried me when I was first born.

We all sing in the church. Mama brought singing home with her. I can hear singing in the kitchen like a bird when we all get to heaven.

Won't it be wonderful there; many more songs; I listen to her sing most of the time.

You could find me in the yard playing.

These are the memories I cannot forget. Mama praying.

Mama would pray, and she got an answer.

She would be on her knees for hours and read her Bible every day.

Back to the time, Mama was talking about this family.

They had so many kids. It was church night then Mama and daddy had to leave. Some of the kids were left at home.

While they're gone, someone knocked at the door. The kids ran to the door. It was a man. They welcomed him and the picture caught his eyes.

He was telling the kids about Jesus, then he left. The kids looked outside and he was gone.

When the family got home, mother was so happy, she shouted.

She knew it was an angel sent by God to protect her children.

Mama did not tell us about her childhood.

My grandfather passed away before I was born.

My grandmother lost some of her children.

My Mama had to play with her brothers like me.

Grandma keeps things hidden inside of her.

Just a few things she told me, like her maiden name. I know we were poor people.

We lived in Grandma's old house. No electric. It was never painted. The water was from a well. No bathroom inside. If we did not get our water from the well before night, we had to carry flash light.

I was afraid to go outside after dark.

Sometimes, God had that old moon bright for us to see where we were going.

We went to bed early. Got up when we heard the rooster crow.

We had no television or anything to keep us awake.

Mama made sure we said our prayers at night time.

The next morning, it was school time. Could not be late.

The school bus would not wait for us.

One day, I saw the bus at the top of the hill. I cried because I knew it was my fault and Mama would not like it.

She would see me coming home dragging in like an old hound dog.

I would try to make up for it and go into the kitchen. Get a stool. Wash the dishes in that old dishpan.

Instead of giving me what I deserved, Mama had me.

She knew the house would be clean.

I had a very good Mama. I thank God every day for giving me her.

I missed her so much.

I think about the title of my book.

With God, Without God.

When I'm at home, I do what Mama wanted me to do.

God was number one in Mama's life. She loved him so much.

The one thing my brother and me liked was Christmas.

We did not get much but what we did get was what we liked.

We liked the snow. We watched it fall on the ground from the window.

Everything would be covered.

I did not like the cold weather, but you take the bad with the good.

I did not have a sister to grow up with.

She got married when I was a little girl. Her name was Rose.

She was older than me. France was younger than me.

God took her when she was very young. My sister Rose, later I will see them one day. I am sure in heaven.

After France got killed in Chicago, her and her friend Barbra walked across the street. A big truck hit them.

I went to stay with daddy in the windy state.

Maxine put me in school.

I met a girl Name Carol.

I was staying the night with Carol when a man broke into our house. He told Maxine's daddy wanted money.

She told him my dad was at work. It was a lie.

We do not know what would happen.

After that my brother sled on the reel in the hall, this man was scared he left.

Daddy went to court; nothing happened.

Carol and I went to the drug store many times.

We played together. We live on the same street.

My little sister got run over in front of our window.

I live there for around two years.

One day after work, daddy come in and said, "let's pack. We are leaving to go to Alabama".

He took me to Grandma's house, his Mama I did not like.

I wanted to live with my Mama and Grandma. I missed my family.

One day I ran away going to see Mama and Grandma.

Johnson and I hid, and they did not find me.

After they left, Grandma said I had to go back. I did.

Later on, Grandma passed away.

I rode the bus by the church. Got off to be at Grandma's funeral.

I think Grandma got mad. Later on, she took me to Mama.

I was so happy to see my family.

I felt so bad losing my Grandma. She was my world.

She made me some dresses when my birthday came around.

She gave me money to buy what I wanted.

She loved the Lord so much.

One day I will see her. I know.

Now I want to go further into my future.

I did not have any nice clothes.

I did not have shoes for my feet. I was made fun at school.

Before Grandma passed, I would come home crying and she would hold me telling me they were jealous of me because I was so pretty.

She had words that made me feel better. After that everything was okay.

When Grandma passed, I felt like I was all by myself.

So along she would take the pain away.

So one day, I quit school.

The cops pick me up. They put me in jail for not going to school.

I stayed there for a while until they had room for me at the training school for girls.

I was so scared. Lots of girls put me in a room and locked it at night.

It was nice there. I learn some things like cooking, cleaning our room, and washing our clothes.

We got to go outside after we were there for a while.

Saturday night after moving, we had a candy bar and at Christmas, we got lots of things from different people.

I went to school. Made my first dress. We had a skating ring. We had fun there.

We pass the television around.

There were three cottages at the train-ing School. We made everything from scratch.

My Mama came one time to take me off for the weekend.

I really like that the weekend went by so fast. She bought me things to take back to the school.

I did go to church with a lady. She come to the school and pick me up. She was really nice.

I did miss my Mama.

She wrote me letters. I was glad to re-ceive them. She told me I would get out soon. She had faith in God.

I would tell her, "no Mama," I was there for a while.

I got a mail from a preacher

Mother gave him my address.

I was like any other kid growing up who did not believe mother. I wanted to.

I know God took care of us kids.

I was there for almost seventeen months.

When I came up for parole, I was scared that I will not be coming home. They asked me questions about what I learned. I told them the best I could. I did have few surprises on my journey.

When I left there, they forgot to tell me that I was not going to my mother's. They're taking me to a foster home.

I stayed there for some time. They were nice people and had good meals to eat.

I got to pick cotton with them.

They had two little kids. They were so cute. They finally got word.

My mother was in Florida with my two brothers.

The people I stayed with did not want me to go.

I was ready to go into my future. The worker put me on the grayhound headed south. I did not know what was in store for my future. It did not look too bright because I had no address. No way but the dear Lord to get me to Florida.

I sat on the bus, just looking around to see if anyone was looking at me. I was seventeen years old. I have never been to Florida before. I guess I will be okay.

My mother and brothers were there.

It had been so long since I had seen them. I got to the Bus stop. I did not know where I was.

The two ladies helped me see if I had my mother's address in my case, I did not have one.

God was smiling down on me that day because as I stepped outside, I saw my brother coming down the sidewalk.

He knew it was me.

He told me I was early. They were looking for me.

Later I was happy to be there.

I was not far away from where mother was. She was waiting on me to get there even though she knew I would be later on coming to her doorsteps. I can see her waiting for me walking through the house, saying where is my baby girl at. I know she prayed for me because when she saw me coming, she ran to meet me.

So happy to see me; it had been so long.

You could see the smile on my face. My little brother was happy too. We had so much to talk about my future.

My mother and my brothers went to church on 441 which has been lots of years.

It is where they have funerals now,

Have seen so many of my own family there to say bye to them. Telling them that I will see them again in heaven.

My mother had many friends that went to the same church. One of them had a daughter named Brenda. She became my dose friend.

We did things together. That is how I met the father of my loving children.

We were married for eight years.

We just could not get along even though we did have time to go to church.

Before we got married, we had a good time.

I give God, my mother, and my brother Raymond credit, my mother.

When I brought anyone to our house, she talked to them about the Lord.

I never understood what mother was saying. I hate to say this, but it embarrassed me at that time, but mother did not care. She would preach to me. I am happy she did.

Mother loved the Lord. She let everyone know it. That is how I feel now.

It hurts me to know there are so many people that do not love Jesus. They think they have more time than the preacher told them.

I know different. I pray for sinners. I hope God lead them the right way.

Get their house in order before the rapture.

We do not have much longer Jesus did not promise us anytime.

It puts tears in my eyes when I know so many people are going to hell.

I thank God every day for the ones who pray for me.

My mother and Grandma are on the top list of thanks.

When my mother passed away, later on in my life I wondered who will pray for me since mother is gone.

That is when my world stops turning.

I change my life. The devil had me in his web. I did not care anymore. I lost my mother. Had nightmares for many years.

After she was gone, I started drinking, smoking, and did things that was wrong.

If Jesus had come been left behind, sad to say.

Thank God for watching over me. Keeping me safe when I did not care I was wrong.

God loves me just the same. I was really deep in sin. Lost all the morals of my life.

Did not think about what mother taught me. I did not care.

Did not want the memories to come back. I had buried them in my soul.

All along with what my mother had taught me, telling me what to do, I was going in the wrong direction.

To lose the good things

I was always to remember

It was not anything for me to go to sleep.

Forget the day.

I miss my mother so much.

I was all along my husband. I was married for eight years. Left the kids and me.

I do not blame him for everything. I had myself to blame as well.

Marrying so young, my mother tried to tell me not to jump into the frying pan into the fire. I did not listen.

I just wanted someone to love me. No one could break that chain bound to me except Jesus.

I was running from him. It was so much different since mother was gone. I just stay in that hole of sin. I had buried myself in it and it swallowed me whole.

Sinking so low, I did not try to get out.

I lost my confidence and tried to lose anyone that wanted to get near me because of my little girls.

I did not want anyone in my life for good.

Did not trust them. I had heard of step-dad bothering other children and not mind. I would not let that happen.

If I was left alone for the rest of my life, it did not pass my mind. I love my kids.

The devil doesn't care if you want to go to church as long as you keep doing his work.

I was not thinking 'about myself is part of without God.

I did things I was not proud of. I could not start over, could not go back.

I did try to be a person that wants to go to church, living the best I could.

I met Jerry, my next husband.

A friend told me about him.

His wife left him and two small children for another man. We married in 1974. I don't think we belong together. His children would not let him forget their mother, and no one could blame them. They wanted their mother and dad together.

It did not change anything. He left me for another woman then I went on with my life.

In 1984, I started up another love.

Lived with a man from Georgia. His name is Bud. He just came out of the army from 68 to 72. I met him in 1973.

He wanted to stay with his dad. His mom passed away in 1973.

We went to Georgia he stayed.

We got married. We were married for 22 years.

I was going thought so much with him. He was drunk most of our time together. I never saw him come home without him all booze up.

I cried so many times and prayed for him to change.

We were separated most of our marriage. He was under doctor care before he passed away.

I want to go back to when I went out. I did not feel good about myself.

I made it home. He wanted to tell me about myself.

I need to change my life. He said God told him to tell me.

I felt the spirit of God. I knew it was true what he was saying.

Sorry to admit it, but I had been playing around with God. Now I had to stop and mean business with him.

I cannot hold on to the enemy and God at the same time. It would not work so I told Bud. He said if I change, he will leave me. I told him he had to leave.

While we were at his sisters', we both prayed every night. He was so proud of me for changing, telling everyone I had changed, getting back where I left off.

We moved in with my daughter Alice.

We were there for a while. He got worse. We put him in a VA hospital.

He was there a little bit.

He went to a nursing home. That is where it all began. He pulls his feeding tube out of his stomach. He was sent back to the hospital. That was 2006 he passed away.

September the 10th, one month later, Alice, my daughter, passed away.

So my world stood still. I put my trust in Jesus. He has pulled US through it all.

I could not go one day without him. I moved on with my life.

Sister Ruth told me about my next husband, Ricky Dobbs. We were together in Apopka. I told him about my friends Sue and Jerry Farmer on our way to Wildwood. We all got along okay. We went to church together, and did some things we like to do.

He asked me to marry him, and I said yes. He bought my rings. We set a date for May 16. We had started back to Apopka.

Sue called me about a house. We looked at it and liked it.

Our first house. We got married and all our plans were carried out by Sister Ruth.

Was so good to help us. We have been married for 9 years now

I do not want to stop here. We live there for some time. We got us two dogs. I named my dog Patty and Ricky's dog lit.

Ricky, we all went to Alabama. We move in with my Sister, daughter and stay for a while. The storms made me change my mind.

We came back to Florida in 2012. God was with us again. We move into a motel. Our friends again found us a place to live.

We have been in one room for B years. Before the air condition went out, we lost our two dogs in 2017. I miss them so much.

Little Ricky went missing. He has been gone for some time. I feel like he is with Patty in heaven.

One day I will see them again. Later on, we pray to the Lord to give us Buddy and another Patty.

She won't take the other one's place, but she is my Baby.

When I brought her home, I took a change. Put her leash on her she, broke loose and ran away, scared me I prayed, please Lord do not I.et anything happen to her. Jesus was with me, he had the devil people to help me find her.

I had been sick that week, so weak. Thank God I got her back. She has her Potty sheets so she does not go. We have found us a church we go to.

We love the people there. They are so nice just because I am writing about my life. I want people that read my book you have time to get ready before the rapture.

Ricky and I found us a Church we love so much. We have been going there for some time. We love the people. We feel at home there.

The people are really nice, the pastor Preacher God's words. Beth, his wife, is really nice to everyone. She loves the Lord.

I want people to know if you read my book. They have time to get ready.

Jesus is coming. I have books online about the rapture. Remember, you may have a mother or a dad in heaven waiting on you, do not disappoint them.

I am so glad I turn my life around. I have a husband who goes to church with me.

One day, I will see my family in heaven, don't you want to do that?

Repeat after, me dear Jesus, I am a sinner. Please forgive me of all my sins 'come into my heart to live. I will confess you to others. Amen

I need to go back when I was a little girl.

My Grandma loved me so much. If I was sick, she would hold me and pray for me.

When it was Saturday night, Grandma would put rolls in my hair. The next morning, she would comb it out for church.

I would cry. She had a word for me, 'do not let the rats sleep in your hair', Grandma no rats sleep in my hair.

I did not like it when she combed my hair, she pulled it out, it would hurt.

That was my Grandma. She was a sweet woman. She loved the Lord.

I remember when she would eat, no teeth. She could eat like a beaver. Nothing was too hard for her.

I wonder how she did it.

My Grandma loved to bake us cookies, cakes and anything she could cook on that old wood stove.

I love to watch her go to the garden, and get fresh vegetables for us to eat.

When she was at our home, we never went hungry. She came there on the first of the month to get her check.

It was good to see her. She brought me something every time she came.

She did not put her money in a bank, and she carried it on her.

The house I was born in, you could see it from the yard. I played with my brother Wallace, and we played together.

If we got into a fight, it was time out from one another.

We did not like that. I like picking blackberries. Mother would make us a pie.

When it snows, we had snow cream. Not anymore. The snow is bad now.

Walking to church would hurt my feet. These things now are so much different than when I was growing up.

Instead of colored television, I saw a black and white one.

After school when my chores were done, then we went to the neighbor's house. We watch western. It was okay for me; I just wanted to go somewhere to play with other kids. We were told by Mama before dark to come home.

We still played after we all watched television.

Remember one day I did not want to go to school? My sister stops by. She made a big thing out of me out of school. It made me mad, said something about it. She chases me down to the grapevine. I step on a piece of glass, wow that hurt.

The blood was dripping everywhere in the house.

Mother pray for me. It put a sore on my foot after it quit bleeding. Mother was sorry I got hurt.

God was with us all the time. When it was stormy weather, it could get bad, we did not have lights.

We had a lamp. That old house could stand anything. Just put some boards put together. You could her the wind outside, blowing it would last for a while. Just rain, I could sleep like a Baby on that old tin top, just rain.

Grandma made me pretty dresses not like hers. She had hers special made. I went with her one time to the house of the woman made her nice dresses.

My Grandma's clothes were most like long to her feet up to her neck. She never wore pants or shorts.

Any coffee and tea, any television at my brothers, they did have a little black and white one.

She asked them to turn it off when she undressed.

I do not remember too much about Grandma. I was a little girl not thinking of an older person except when I needed something. Sorry to say that she spoils me. You know we may have been poor, but we had the love that is something you cannot buy.

My Mama loves us and my Grandma. She was someone to fill in for Mama.

When she was sick, she stood in to take care of us.

Mama was in the field lots picking cotton. Grandma, I never saw her in the cotton fields. She may have brought mama water.

It was so bad in the fields. If you did not hurt your knees, your hands would hurt

Mama, would drag that old sack across the cotton patch so tired, but she had to fill daddy's shoes and take care of us kids.

That she went into the woods for firewood so we would have a warm room to get up in.

When we went to School, Mama made the fire first thing in the morning. In Alabama, it stays cold.

We live in the north pan of the state where hills meet hill and carve meets carve, where people pray for hours on their knees, where Neighbors help each other, and where Churches are everywhere.

The old county store mama would go to buy us grocers. I can see her coming down the road. Her dress swung in the wind.

Back then, people thought about God morning, noon, and night. If people now had to do what we did back then.

I do not know how they would stand it.

God was with us many times. Our cow ate some poison, Mama pray for her, we got milk the next day.

I met one of my friends at my Mama's friends. We were all going to church. Her grandmother was the one she lived with close.

It was the first time I wore a pretty dress. She let me wear one of her dresses. I felt like a different person

My clothes were hand me downs and what Mama and Grandma made me out of flour sack.

We walked to the church many times.

There were other people walked with us. Peggy and I sat on the same seat. We had to be quiet.

Mama would get me when I got home if I was loud in church.

The pastor of the church, he preaches for a long time no watch. We all went home when it was over.

Every time the church was open, we went. Mama never left us home unless when were sick, then someone stayed with us. God was with us. We never had to worry about someone coming to our school with a gun.

We prayed at night and Mama was always praying lots on her knees.

She had a few friends that lived by us, Mrs. Fanny King and Mrs. Bevers.

There were some at church Mama Friends. I was a little girl, so I do not remember too much about what happened. We lived on a mountain. You could see Stevenson, Alabama from our house.

We sometime would go down the mountain to the river. One thing I remember was a rock

That had a footprint on top of it. I was up there in 2011.

It was there when I was a little girl. After I left, I went back and could not find it.

I was thinking of taking a picture of it. I do not know what happened to it

I was there in 2011 when the storms were bad. I found out something after you leave, you cannot go back, not the same Mama gone, my brothers are gone, the house is on the ground.

Just lots of memories left in that old house.

I found a little ball, and I played with it. I was like a boy. All I had to play with was boys except when my kin came.

From Florida, there we play almost night. I miss my family. I know they are in heaven, see them.

I am so glad I came from a family that loves the Lord.

I remember one day when we thought a man had broken out of jail. They had it on the news.

We had to lock our doors. It was something we never had to worry about.

I went to spend the night with one of my friends from school. We had so much fun. Their family made candy. I was surprised that mother let me go.

That was the only time she let me go. I did miss my family.

Never been away from home before. I got in trouble one time when I went with my aunt sister to Tenn. my mother did not know where I was. I stay the night. I did not tell my mother, I just left.

Mother was worried. Well, that is enough about me and my life in the end.

The most important thing about my life is what happened to me when I was a toddler crawling around on the floor. I saw the kerosene can, I put it up and drank some of it.

My brother Raymond saw what I had done. He calls to mother's attention. She picked me up and prayed for me. It was so many years ago. Since then, Raymond has been preaching. He told in his services that I was a miracle baby. Mother had faith God healed me because mother said I looked as white as a piece of cotton when she picked me up. You cannot outdo God.

He is a healer. He is a provider. He is a miracle worker.

He is a Resurrection. He can the only way to heaven is through Jesus Christ, my Lord

ABOUT THE AUTHOR

I was born in north Alabama in the late '40s. I came to Florida in 1960. That's where I start my little family. I'm a born-again Christian. And I have been writing books since 2009. I am a passionate writer. I also write songs and poems. I started to establish influential author and hardly believed in God.